LIFE IS

Quotes about life and its meaning, said over the ages by the greats, and some not-so-greats too

Mil Media

Collated by N. G. Blum

Designed by Roshe Granite

copyright © 2014 by Mil-media *mil*

Contents

Prolog

Who among us hasn't sighed happily in a moment of bliss, This is the life? Or wondered during a moment of contemplation, What is the meaning of life?

What is life? Is it a magical journey of poignant sensations? Is it just a grinding road to an inevitable end? Can life truly be compared to a car, or a cake?

Maybe all the answers we found are right, or maybe they're utter nonsense. In any case the question seems to have preoccupied man going back to the dawn of time. Answers are legion, from the light-hearted to the leaden. And sometimes you find answers delivered with the weightiest intent to be hysterically funny.

We too embarked on a quest to find answers to the ultimate question – What is life? We collated hundreds of suggestions and have put together the best for you, divided by category.

Some are inspiring, some perhaps less so; take it as a collection of quips, philosophical thoughts or even as a motivational morés to help you get a lot more out of life.

—

Life is Hard

Life is tough,
but it's tougher
when you're stupid

John Wayne

—

To the wise,
life is a problem;
to the fool, a solution

Marcus Aurelius

—

The difficulty in life
is the choice

George Moore, The Bending of the Bough

Life is full of misery,
loneliness, and suffering
and it's all over
much too soon

Woody Allen

—

When life is too easy
for us, we must beware
or we may not be ready
to meet the blows
which sooner or later
come to everyone,
rich or poor

Eleanor Roosevelt

Life is never easy
for those who dream

Robert James Waller

—

Life is just one damned
thing after another

Elbert Hubbard

—

When I hear somebody
sigh, 'Life is hard,' I am always
tempted to ask,
'Compared to what?'

Sydney J. Harris

Life is hard. Then you die.
Then they throw dirt
in your face.
Then the worms eat you.
Be grateful it happens
in that order

David Gerrold

—

Life is very interesting...
in the end, some of your
greatest pains become your
greatest strengths

Drew Barrymore

Life is thickly sown with
thorns, and I know no other
remedy than to pass quickly
through them.
The longer we dwell on our
misfortunes, the greater is
their power to harm us

Voltaire

—

Life is hard.
After all, it kills you

Katharine Hepburn

—

Life is an improv act

Life is a moderately good play with a badly written third act

Truman Capote

Life is the art of drawing without an eraser

John W. Gardner

Life is the art of drawing sufficient conclusions from insufficient premises

Samuel Butler

Life is like dancing.
If we have a big floor,
many people will dance.
Some will get angry when
the rhythm changes.
But life is changing
all the time

Miguel Angel Ruiz

—

Life is like a trumpet -
if you don't put anything
into it, you don't get
anything out of it

William Christopher Handy

Life is a lot like jazz...
it's best when
you improvise

George Gershwin

—

Life is like a beautiful
melody, only the lyrics
are messed up

Hans Christian Andersen

—

Life is one grand,
sweet song,
so start the music

Ronald Reagan

Life is the art of being well
deceived, and to succeed,
it must be habitual and
uninterrupted

Oscar Wilde

—

Life is a great big canvas,
and you should throw all the
paint on it you can

Danny Kaye

—

Life doesn't imitate art,
it imitates bad television

Woody Allen

Life is like a novel.
It's filled with suspense.
You have no idea what
is going to happen until
you turn the page

Sidney Sheldon

The fairness of Life

Life is not fair;
get used to it

Bill Gates

—

Life is never fair,
and perhaps it is a good
thing for most of us
that it is not

Oscar Wilde

Life is fair.
We all get the same
nine-month shake in the
box, and then the dice roll.
Some people get
a run of sevens.
Some people, unfortunately,
get snake-eyes.
Its just how the world is

Stephen King, Full Dark, No Stars

—

Life is a rubber band

Life is a game
and true love is a trophy

Rufus Wainwright, Poses

—

O excellent!
I love long life
better than figs

William Shakespeare,
Antony and Cleopatra

—

Life is a paradise for
those who love many things
with a passion

Leo Buscaglia

Life is the flower for which
love is the honey

Victor Hugo

—

Life is a series of pulls
back and forth...
A tension of opposites, like
a pull on a rubber band.
Most of us live
somewhere in the middle.
A wrestling match...
Which side win?
Love wins. Love always wins

Mitch Albom,
Tuesdays With Morrie

—

Life is short

Life is short,
Break the rules.
Forgive quickly,
Kiss slowly.
Love truly.
Laugh uncontrollably
and never regret
anything that
makes you smile

Mark Twain

—

Life is half spent before
we know what it is

George Herbert

Life is much shorter than I imagined it to be

Abraham Cahan

—

Be patient and understanding. Life is too short to be vengeful or malicious

Phillips Brooks

—

Life is short, yet sweet

Euripides

The life so short, the craft so long to learn

Hippocrates

—

Life is short, so enjoy it to the fullest...

Spider Robinson

—

Life is too short when you think of the length of death

Sean Mangan

Life is too short,
or too long, for me to
allow myself the luxury
of living it so badly

Paulo Coelho

—

Life is not measured by
the time we live

George Crabbe, Village

—

Life can't happen to you

Life is not a matter of
holding good cards,
but of playing a
poor hand well

Robert Louis Stevenson

—

Life is a barter
of choice and consequences

Samantha Sotto, Before Ever After

—

Life is like a game of tables,
the chances are not in our
power, but the playing is

Terence, Adelphi

Life is 10 percent what
you make it, and 90 percent
how you take it

Irving Berlin

—

Life is 10 percent what
happens to you
and 90 percent how
you respond to it

Lou Holtz

Life is a gamble.
You can get hurt,
but people die
in plane crashes,
lose their arms and
legs in car accidents;
people die every day.
Same with fighters:
some die, some get hurt,
some go on.
You just don't
let yourself believe
it will happen to you

Muhammad Ali

Life is simple

Life is not complex.
We are complex.
Life is simple,
and the simple
thing is the
right thing

Oscar Wilde

———

Life is not what it's
supposed to be.
It's what it is.
The way you cope
with it is what makes
the difference

Virginia Satir

Life is pretty simple:
You do some stuff.
Most fails. Some works.
You do more of what works.
If it works big,
others quickly copy it.
Then you do something else.
The trick is the doing
something else

Leonardo da Vinci

—

Life is really simple,
but we insist on making
it complicated

Confucius

—

Life is to be enjoyed

Life is far too important a thing ever to talk seriously about

Oscar Wilde

—

Life is not a problem to be solved, but a reality to be experienced

Soren Kierkegaard

—

Life is to be enjoyed, not endured

Gordon B. Hinckley

Life is ours to be spent,
not to be saved

D.H. Lawrence

—

Life is a comedy
to those who think,
a tragedy
to those who feel

Jean Racine

The end of Life

Life is a
great sunrise.
I do not see
why death
should not be an
even greater one

Vladimir Nabokov

—

Life is pleasant.
Death is peaceful.
It's the transition
that's troublesome

Isaac Asimov

Eternity is a very long time,
especially towards the end

Woody Allen

—

Life is better than death,
I believe, if only because
it is less boring,
and because it has fresh
peaches in it

Alice Walker

—

Don't cry because it's over,
smile because it happened

Dr. Seuss

Life is a disease: sexually transmitted, and invariably fatal

Neil Gaiman

—

Life is a predicament which precedes death

Henry James

—

Death is Certain, Life is not

Augustus Hill, Oz

Life is like a
concentration camp...
you can't leave
without dying

Woody Allen

—

Life is rather
a state of embryo,
a preparation for life;
a man is not completely
born till he has
passed through death

Benjamin Franklin

I intend to live forever, or die trying

Groucho Marx

—

If birth is a manifestation of life, death is another

Dejan Stojanovic

—

Life is the bumble bee
and the rain

My life is my message

Mahatma Gandhi

—

The meaning of life
is that it stops

Franz Kafka

—

What do you want
a meaning for?
Life is a desire,
not a meaning

Charlie Chaplin

Our life is nothing but
a winter's day;
Some only break their
fast, and so away:
Others stay to dinner,
and depart full fed:
The deepest age but
sups, and goes to bed:
He's most in debt that
lingers out the day:
Who dies betime, has less,
and less to pay

Francis Quarles, Divine Fancies,
On The Life of Man

Life is not measured
by the breaths we take
but by the moments that
take our breath away

Hilary Cooper

—

Believe that life is
worth living and your belief
will help create the fact

William James

—

Our life is what
our thoughts make it

Marcus Aurelius

Life is full of beauty.
Notice it.
Notice the bumble bee,
the small child,
and the smiling faces.
Smell the rain,
and feel the wind.
Live your life to the
fullest potential, and

fight for your dreams

Ashley Smith

—

A useless life
is an early death

Johann Wolfgang von Goethe,
Iphigenia auf Tauris

Life is a mission.
Every other definition
of life is false,
and leads all
who accept it astray.
Religion, science,
philosophy, though still
at variance upon many
points, all agree in this,
that every existence
is an aim

Mazzini, Life and Writings

—

Life is but thought

Sara Teasdale

My point is,
life is about balance.
The good and the bad.
The highs and the lows.
The pina and the colada

Ellen DeGeneres, Seriously...I'm Kidding

—

The purpose of life is the
expansion of happiness

Deepak Chopra

—

Life is either a daring
adventure or nothing at all

Helen Keller

Life is one big road with
lots of signs. So when you
riding through the ruts, don't
complicate your mind.
Flee from hate,
mischief and jealousy.
Don't bury your thoughts,
put your vision to reality.
Wake Up and Live!

Bob Marley

—

Life isn't about
finding yourself. Life is about
creating yourself

George Bernard Shaw

The great object of life is
sensation - to feel that we exist,
even though in pain

George Gordon Byron

—

We don't get a chance
to do that many things,
and every one should
be really excellent.
Because this is our life.
Life is brief, and then
you die, you know?
So this is what we've
chosen to do with our life

Steve Jobs

Life is for living backwards

In my next life I want to
live my life backwards.
You start out dead and get that
out of the way.
Then you wake up in an
old people's home feeling better
every day.
You get kicked out for
being too healthy,
go collect your pension,
and then when you start work,
you get a gold watch and
a party on your first day.
You work for 40 years until
you're young enough
to enjoy your retirement.

You party, drink alcohol, and are generally promiscuous, then you are ready for high school. You then go to primary school, you become a kid, you play. You have no responsibilities, you become a baby until you are born. And then you spend your last 9 months floating in luxurious spa-like conditions with central heating and room service on tap, larger quarters every day and then Voila! You finish off as an orgasm!

Woody Allen

Life, too, is like that.
You live it forward, but
understand it backward

Abraham Verghese

—

Life is a succession
of lessons which must be
lived to be understood

Ralph Waldo Emerson

—

Life is uncharted territory.
It reveals its story one
moment at a time

Leo Buscaglia

Life is a culmination
of the past, an awareness
of the present, an indication
of a future beyond
knowledge, the quality
that gives a touch of
divinity to matter

Charles Lindbergh

—

Life is a series of
collisions with the future;
it is not the sum
of what we have been,
but what we yearn to be

Jose Ortega y Gasset

Life is about not knowing,
having to change,
taking the moment and
making the best of it,
without knowing what's
going to happen

Gilda Radner

—

To know nothing
is the happiest life

Desiderius Erasmus

—

Life is making the world
a better place

A life is not important
except in the impact it has
on other lives

Jackie Robinson

—

Only a life lived for others
is a life worthwhile

Albert Einstein

—

Human life is but
a series of footnotes
to a vast obscure
unfinished masterpiece

Vladimir Nabokov, Lolita

Life is a long lesson in humility

James M. Barrie

—

Life is an exciting business, and most exciting when it is lived for others

Helen Keller

—

Life is funny

Life is a tragedy
when seen in close-up,
but a comedy in long-shot

Charlie Chaplin

—

Life is a beautiful
magnificent thing,
even to a jellyfish

Charlie Chaplin

—

Life is something
that everyone should try
at least once

Henry J. Tillman

Man does not control his own fate. The women in his life do that for him

Groucho Marx

—

Life is a sexually transmitted disease and the mortality rate is one hundred percent

R. D. Laing

—

Life is wasted on the living

Douglas Adams

Life is something to do
when you can't get to sleep

Fran Lebowitz

—

Life is such a glorious
trauma, is it not?

J.R. Ward, Lover Avenged

—

Life does not cease to be
funny when people die any
more than it ceases to be
serious when people laugh

George Bernard Shaw

Life is anything that dies
when you stomp on it

Dave Barry

—

You can live to be a hundred
if you give up all the things
that make you want to live
to be a hundred

Woody Allen

—

If you can fake that,
you've got it made

Groucho Marx

My one regret in life is that
I am not someone else

Woody Allen

—

Life is made up of sobs,
sniffles, and smiles,
with sniffles
predominating

O. Henry

—

Beer: The cause of,
and solution to,
all of life's problems

Homer Simpson

Life is a foreign language; all men mispronounce it

Christopher Morley

—

The answer to life's problems aren't at the bottom of a bottle, they're on TV!

Homer Simpson

—

All my life I've had one dream, to achieve my many goals

Homer Simpson

The three little sentences
that will get you through life.
No' 1: Cover for me.
No' 2: Oh, good idea, Boss!
No' 3: It was like that
when I got here

Homer Simpson

———

Son, if you really want
something in this life, you
have to work for it.
Now quiet!
They're about to announce
the lottery numbers

Homer Simpson

—

Life is cynical

Life is what happens while you are busy making other plans

John Lennon

—

Life is as tedious as a twice-told tale, Vexing the dull ear of a drowsy man

William Shakespeare, King John

—

Life is more or less a lie, but then again, that's exactly the way we want it to be

Bob Dylan

Life is essentially
a cheat and its conditions
are those of defeat;
the redeeming things are
not happiness and pleasure
but the deeper satisfactions
that come out of struggle

F. Scott Fitzgerald

—

Life contains but
two tragedies.
One is not to get your
heart's desire;
the other is to get it

George Bernard Shaw

I feel that life is divided into the horrible and the miserable. That's the two categories. The horrible are like, I don't know, terminal cases, you know, and blind people, crippled.
I don't know how they get through life. It's amazing to me. And the miserable is everyone else.
So you should be thankful that you're miserable, because that's very lucky, to bemiserable

Woody Allen, Annie Hall

Life is not meant to be an open-book test

Alyson Noel

—

Life is a peephole, a single tiny entry onto a vastness - how can I not dwell on this brief, cramped view of things? This peephole is all I've got!

Yann Martel, Life of Pi

Life is like...

Life is a dream for the wise,
a game for the fool,
a comedy for the rich,
a tragedy for the poor

Sholom Aleichem

—

Life is a mirror and will reflect
back to the thinker what he
thinks into it

Ernest Holmes

—

Life is a crazy ride,
and nothing is guaranteed

Eminem

Life is a shipwreck,
but we must not forget
to sing in the lifeboat

Voltaire

—

Life is not like water.
Things in life don't
necessarily flow over the
shortest possible route

Haruki Murakami, 1Q84

—

Life is only a flicker
of melted ice

Dejan Stojanovic

Life is a pure flame,
and we live by an invisible
sun within us

Sir Thomas Browne, Hydriotaphia

—

Life is like riding a bicycle.
To keep your balance,
you must keep moving

Albert Einstein

—

Life is like therapy -
real expensive and
no guarantees

Garth Brooks

My momma always said life was
like a box of chocolates. You
never know what
you're gonna get

Forrest Gump

—

Life is a bowl of cherries.
Some cherries are rotten
while others are good;
its your job to throw out
the rotten ones and forget
about them while you
enjoy eating the ones
that are good!

C. JoyBell C.

Life is like an onion;
you peel it off one layer
at a time, and sometimes
you weep

Carl Sandburg

—

Life is a smoke that curls -
Curls in a flickering skein,
That winds and whisks and
whirls, A figment thin and
vain, Into the vast inane.
One end for hut and hall

William Ernest Henley,
Of the Nothingness of Things

—

Life is career

My secret to a long,
healthy life is to always
keep working.
It keeps me busy
and happy,
and gives me a reason
to stay alive

Johannes Heesters

—

You should not confuse your
career with your life

Dave Barry

Life is too short
to work so hard

Vivien Leigh

—

For me life is
continuously being hungry.
The meaning of life
is not simply to exist,
to survive, but to
move ahead, to go up,
to achieve, to conquer

Arnold Schwarzenegger

Life is to experiment

Life is a series of natural
and spontaneous changes.
Don't resist them -
that only creates sorrow.
Let reality be reality.
Let things flow naturally
forward in whatever
way they like

Lao Tzu

—

Life is a succession
of moments, to live each
one is to succeed

Corita Kent

Your life is the fruit of your own doing. You have no one to blame but yourself

Joseph Campbell

—

Life is divided into three terms - that which was, which is, and which will be. Let us learn from the past to profit by the present, and from the present, to live better in the future

William Wordsworth

A life spent making mistakes is not only more honorable, but more useful than a life spent doing nothing

George Bernard Shaw

—

Life is a succession of lessons which must be lived to be understood

Helen Keller

Life is a series of
experiences, each one
of which makes us bigger,
even though sometimes it
is hard to realize this.
For the world was built to
develop character,
and we must learn that
the setbacks and grieves
which we endure help us
in our marching onward

Henry Ford

All life is an experiment. The more experiments you make the better

Ralph Waldo Emerson

———

Life is to be conflicted

Life is, in fact, a battle.
Evil is insolent and strong;
beauty enchanting, but rare;
goodness very apt to be weak;
folly very apt to be defiant;
wickedness to carry the day;
imbeciles to be in great
places, people of sense in
small, and mankind generally
unhappy. But the world as it
stands is no narrow illusion,
no phantasm, no evil dream
of the night; we wake up to it,
forever and ever; and we can
neither forget it nor deny it
nor dispense with it

Henry James, Theory of Fiction: Henry James

The web of our life is of a mingled yarn, good and ill together

William Shakespeare,
All's Well That Ends Well

—

Life is neither good nor evil, but only a place for good and evil

Marcus Aurelius

www.ingramcontent.com/pod-product-compliance
Lightning Source LLC
Chambersburg PA
CBHW080421290526
45791CB00008BA/2364